For Charles James

William Collins Sons & Co. Ltd.
London · Glasgow · Sydney · Auckland
Toronto · Johannesburg

First published 1990

© *text compilation Jane Romer 1989*
© *illustrations Emma Chichester Clark 1990*

A CIP catalogue record for this book is
available from the British Library

ISBN 0 00 195443 1

Printed and bound in Hong Kong.

ROCK~A~BYE

BABY

JANE ROMER
Illustrated
by

EMMA CHICHESTER CLARK

COLLINS

Lullaby and Goodnight

Fais Dodo

Rock-a-Bye Baby

Raisins and Almonds

Bei meine kin-de-le's vi - - - ge - le, Schlaff ai klor vi - se
To my lit - tle one's cra -dle in the night, Comes a new lit -tle

tsi - - - ge - le,– Dos tsige-le ist ge-for-en han-dlen, Dos vet tsein
goat so sno-wy white,– The goat will trot to– the mar-ket, Mo-ther her

dei— ba - ruf— Re-schink -e- lech— mit man-dlen. Schloff meine
wa-tch will keep,– To bring you rai-sins and al - monds. Sleep my

ji - de-le, schloff meine ji - de-le, Schloff meine ji - de -le, schloff.
lit- tle one, Sleep my lit- tle one, Sleep my lit- tle one, sleep.

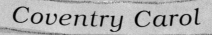

Herod the king in his raging,
Charg-ed he hath this day
His men of might, in his own sight,
All young children to slay.

Then woe is me, poor child, for thee
And ever morn and day
For thy parting nor say, nor sing
Bye Bye lully lullay.

Hush Little Baby

Hush lit-tle ba-by don't you cry Ma-ma's gon-na sing you a lul-la-by,

Hush lit-tle ba-by don't say a word Dad-dy's gon-na buy you a mock-ing bird,

And if that mocking bird won't sing
Mama's gonna buy you a diamond ring,
If that diamond ring turns brass
Daddy's gonna buy you a looking glass,
And if that looking glass gets broke
Ma-ma's gonna buy you a billy goat,
And if that billy goat won't pull
Daddy's gonna buy you a cart and bull,
And if that cart and bull fall down
You'll be the sleepiest little baby in town.

Golden Slumbers

Gol - den slum - bers kiss your eyes,

Smiles a - wake you when you rise,

Sleep pre-tty ba - by do- not cry,– And

I will sing a lul - la - by.

Care is heavy therefore sleep,
Mother is here her watch will keep,
Sleep pretty baby do not cry,
And I will sing a lullaby.

Bajushki Baju

Spi mla-de-nets, moy pre-kra - sni Ba - jush-ki ba - ju,

Tik-ho smo-trit,– mes-iats ia - sni V ko-ly-bel tvoy - u.

Spi mladenets, moy prekrasni
Bajushki baju,
Close your eyes and keep on dreaming,
Bajushki baju.

Sleep my baby, sleep my pretty,
Bajushki baju,
While the moon is shining brightly
From above on you.

I will tell you many stories,
And will sing to you.
Close your eyes and keep on dreaming,
Bajushki baju
Bajushki baju.

Alunde

A - lun-de, a - lun-de, ———— a -lun-de   a - lu-

ya ————   Yee peu wai-yee yee yee Yee peu wa-

ye. ———   A —————————————— lun-de, —

— A ——————————————— lun-de———

Chorus:
Yee peu made qua qua
Qu yee peu waye.
Alunde, Alunde.

Slumberland

Bye Baby Bunting

Bye baby Bunting
Mummy's gone a-milking,
Gone to fetch a milky cup
To fill the baby Bunting up,
Bye baby Bunting.

Bye baby Bunting
Granny's gone a-silking,
To knit a little pair of socks
And a cap for baby's locks,
Bye baby Bunting.

Twinkle, Twinkle Little Star

Twin-kle, twin-kle lit-tle star How I won-der what you are,

Up a-bove the world so high Like a dia-mond in the sky.

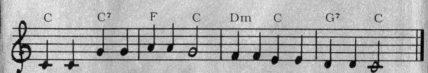

Twin-kle, twin-kle lit-tle star How I won-der what you are.

When the blazing sun is gone,
When he nothing shines upon,
Then you show your little light,
Twinkle, twinkle all the night.

Chorus:

Then the traveller in the dark
Thanks you for your tiny spark,
He could not see which way to go
If you did not twinkle so.

Chorus:

In the dark blue sky you keep
And often through the curtains peep,
For you never shut your eye
Till the sun is in the sky.

Chorus: